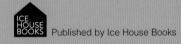 Published by Ice House Books

Written by Samantha Rigby & Raphaella Thompson
Designed by Rhys Kitson

Ice House Books is an imprint of Half Moon Bay Limited
The Ice House, 124 Walcot Street, Bath, BA1 5BG
www.halfmoonbay.co.uk

ISBN 978-1-912867-01-1

Printed in China

Lady Penelope's

BOSS LADY

Handbook

ICE HOUSE BOOKS

Enjoy life's
adventures
and *mysteries.*

"*Isn't life fun sometimes?*"

Remember to take some *time out.*

"I feel I'd be failing in my duties as hostess, if I didn't tell you that in my home, everything stops for tea."

Try to be *considerate* when chasing down one's *enemies.*

> *"Wait for a clear stretch of road, Parker. We don't want to cause a scene."*

Know when it's time to pull out the big guns.

"I had hoped I wouldn't have to go to the ultimate lengths. But they leave me no choice."

Maintain
perspective.

"*Let's forget the whole thing for a moment and drink our coffee.*"

Stall the enemy.

―――――――――――――――――――

*"May I fix my face before I die?
It's in such a mess."*

Take your place on the *team.*

"*I shan't consider myself part of the team until I've been out on a rescue.*"

Prioritise *loyalty* to your allies.

"I always obey the call of friendship, Sir Jeremy."

Praise others *for the skills* they provide.

"*You certainly have a way with safes, Parker. Thank goodness so few people share your talent.*"

Dress up *and go out* whenever the mood takes you.

"Parker, get the Rolls-Royce. We are going for a little drive."

Well-behaved women seldom make history.

"We're heading for trouble."

Remember
to forget
about it all sometimes.

"*Now, that's enough of that for the time being.*"

Involve *yourself* in the action.

"*A little bit of excitement is welcome now and again.*"

Don't
hesitate.

---

*"We've got to work fast.
We are up against men
who will stop at nothing. "*

Get your *priorities* in order.

"Well, come now, Sir Jeremy, it's cocktail time. No one is going to deprive me of my Pernod this time."

Only sweat the *big* stuff.

"Oh, dear. I just hope they don't scratch the paintwork, I'm off to Ascot in the morning."

Make use of your *resources* *and* connections.

"*Oh, I've been around, you know. High society keeps me pretty busy.*"

Maintain awareness
of your opponent's
tactics.

---

*"You mean that bullet was
meant for us?"*

You get out
what you
put in.

"After all, it is my money."

Keep a *composed* headspace.
Balance is key.

"I'm beginning to catch the holiday mood. A little music, Parker?"

Recognise when an *intervention* is needed.

"It's alright, Parker. This doesn't seem to be your night. I'm going to take over."

After a
hard day's work,
unwind
with your colleagues.

"Parker will be along in a minute to take us to the best nightclub in town."

Maintain an air of *mystery.*

"*Mr Ashton, you must allow a lady a few secrets.*"

When *luxury* is in short supply, toughen up.

"Well, never mind. We can get up to the mine on foot."

compliments *are vital in* maintaining *morale.*

"*I must say, Parker,*
you look quite dashing!"

Don't let anyone
underestimate
your abilities.

"Stop worrying about me, Jeff Tracy.
Just be ready for my call."

Snap up
exciting new
opportunities.

"I just can't tell you how thrilled I am to be here."

Always
remember
you are FAB.